ong

David Fulton Publishers Ltd
The Chiswick Centre, 414 Chiswick High Road, London W4 5TF

www.fultonpublishers.co.uk

First published in Great Britain by David Fulton Publishers in association
with the National Association for Special Educational Needs (NASEN)

NASEN is a registered charity no. 1007023.

David Fulton Publishers is a division of Granada Learning Limited, part
of ITV plc.

British Library Cataloguing in Publication Data
A catalogue record for this book is available from the British Library.

ISBN 184312 364 9

Typeset by FiSH Books, London
Printed and bound in Great Britain

Contents

1 Understanding loss

> We are healed of a suffering only by experiencing it to the full.
>
> (Proust, *Albertine disparue*, 1925)

The pain caused by loss is not something that some endure and others escape. We all experience it at some time or other and in different ways, whether it is the huge loss at the death of someone we love or the smaller losses such as the loss of a favourite toy or a friend moving away. Loss is a natural part of life and our reactions to it are equally normal. Children experience different types of loss just as adults do – at home, in the classroom, playground and the community.

This booklet will:

- present a model of loss
- provide an *aide-mémoire* for listening to troubled children
- detail the reactions that children have to the loss of a parent.

It will increase awareness of the meaning of loss to children and show school staff why being there is the essential component of any support we can give a child experiencing the pain caused by loss. But it does not offer simplistic solutions to the emotional reactions which are part of the normal healing process.

There will be rare but extreme and traumatic instances where we will need to turn immediately to external colleagues for advice and support. Such circumstances are when children:

- witness murder
- discover a suicidal parent's body
- talk of self-harm.

We are concerned here, however, with how children cope with the more common instances of loss such as when a parent or carer leaves home or when someone close to them dies.

The key assumption here is that the distress that children experience when a family member dies or when the family breaks down will in some way affect their learning and school life. Because schools are so much part of a child's life it follows that there will be times when a child might wish to talk with someone in school. An understanding of some of the processes and reactions to loss will also enable a school to respond sensitively to any changes in a child's behaviour, attitude or general progress.

As a society it has taken us some time to understand and appreciate the fact that children experience the pain of loss as much as adults do. Children grieve in a different way, and at times they may disguise their grief, but they all have reactions to loss, whether big or small.

This booklet is mostly concerned with the 'big losses' that many children face, namely the death of a grandparent or a parent, and the physical loss of a parent through family breakdown. But it should be emphasised that there are other losses that many children face.

Everyday losses

Children show reactions to a wide range of everyday losses that they experience. In school, examples are:

- when a support/care team member moves
- when a child changes class
- when a friend moves away
- when a child unexpectedly fails a test.

At home, examples are:

- the death of a pet

- the loss of favourite toy
- moving to a new area.

Children with special educational needs struggle with and come to terms with loss each day:

- the child suffering with dyslexia feels the loss of not being able to do what his or her peers find so easy
- the child with physical challenges struggles to keep up with his or her friends
- the child with a hearing impairment feels the loss of not understanding or being understood.

While there is no intention here to argue that school staff should be counsellors, all of us have some everyday understanding of loss. However, this understanding is naturally coloured by our own background – which can contain myths that may be less than helpful (such as the belief that it is best to protect children from the pain of loss). Through exploring the meaning and experience of loss this booklet will help an adult sit a little more confidently with a child who is coping with a loss.

Attachment and loss

We cannot understand loss without first exploring attachment. As infants our survival depends upon an adult taking care of us and to ensure this takes place we are all pre-programmed to attach to a carer. The baby is ready to bond with its carer, while the carer is pre-wired to respond to the needs of a baby. A baby has the innate capacity to communicate its needs: a cry can produce an immediate reaction. Without immediate care babies would be in extreme danger of perishing.

A major contributor to our understanding of the attachment process is John Bowlby (quoted in Holmes, 1995). Bowlby argued that infants are pre-programmed with attachment behaviour which is aimed at maintaining the strong emotional and physical bond between mother and child. Some examples would be clinging to the mother and crying when separated.

BUT when this natural biological bond is broken there are set reactions that occur. This was first detailed in the work of Robertson (Robertson, 1952), a colleague of John Bowlby. Robertson filmed and detailed the reactions of infants when separated from their parents due to hospitalisation. He identified three distinct phases.

- *Phase 1*: Strong reaction, aggressively tearful. The behaviour is attempting to re-establish the relationship as it was.
- *Phase 2*: A mournful period follows. Here the child seems to be grieving the loss.
- *Phase 3*: In this phase the child seems to return to a near normal state where he or she is now able to cope with the loss and continue with his or her life.

There seems to be a natural process that occurs when the biological bond is broken. The first stage is an attempt to re-establish the bond. There is an anger that drives the child and his or her crying is of an angry, screaming type.

If the relationship cannot be re-established there is a 'mourning'-type reaction to the loss, when sadness becomes the dominant emotional response. This phase involves the beginnings of an acceptance of the loss. The crying that occurs now is a much deeper type; the child sobs.

Finally the child moves towards the acceptance of the loss and develops ways of adjusting to a world without the loved one. There is not a 'getting over' the loss, but a coping. We talk of our heart 'being shattered'. This seems to describe how we fall apart and then come back together in a different way now that our world has changed.

One cannot imagine losing a loved person and not having a strong emotional reaction. It would be psychologically contradictory to say that we loved someone and felt nothing at the loss of them. The price of loving is the pain that we feel at their loss.

The reactions that this model suggest are presented in Figure 1.

While this model specifically increases our understanding of how children react to loss through bereavement, it can serve as a useful framework to understand many other losses. The loss of a parent through family breakdown does not have the finality of bereavement, but a child's reaction to it will share many similarities. For example, a child whose father was tragically killed in a farm accident became much more argumentative and disobedient at school, while a girl of eight whose parents were in the middle of an acrimonious divorce became extremely sullen, despondent and complained of being frequently tired. For both children these behaviours were not typical.

STAGE	Protest	Despair	Adjust
Feelings	shock anger denial	sadness, confusion, longing	becoming to terms
Behaviour	arguments and disobedience	tearfulness, loss of sleep and appetite	new friends and activities
Thoughts	I cannot imagine life without them	If only... I would do anything to bring them back	I am still sad, but I can cope
TASK	Accept loss	Experience grief	Adjust and cope

FIGURE 1. Making sense of loss

5

If the reactions are natural, why do children need help? Given that the responses seem to be biologically programmed into us, why do so many children and adults experience difficulties in expressing their grief. The answer lies in the way we are socialised through our family into the dominant cultural values of our time. This is how we learn to avoid emotions that need to be expressed. A useful way to understand this is to think of all of the 'cultural myths' that we learn which are supposed to deal with our emotions, such as:

- be strong
- time will heal
- cheer up
- grieve alone.

The result of these is that many of us find it hard to express how we actually feel. These emotions can then knot up inside and lead to such negative results as:

- behaviour problems
- phobias
- physical illness.

Models of loss

There have been many ways of making sense of severe loss. In the past loss was often seen as a 'one-off' event that children recovered from as well as they could. More recently this was modified to include an understanding of the 'aftershocks' that are felt many times after the actual loss; for example, when a child has to cope with Special Days.

Today it is accepted that significant losses reverberate throughout a person's life. Severe losses in childhood can change the direction in which a child is developing. A lively, outgoing child can become passive and withdrawn if a number of losses are experienced close together. The child's developing personality can be altered in the face of such painful and uncontrollable events. This emphasises the profound effect early losses can have on children and the importance of the way in which they are supported to help them tolerate the sadness the loss causes and to go on to function competently in the real world.

We must remember that the model shown in Figure 1 is a framework to help us understand the process of loss and is not meant to be imposed on children. The experience of grief needs best to be seen as a journey. Some will pass through it relatively quickly. Others will go around roundabouts many times, sometimes entering a cul-de-sac. The average time for a child to come to terms with a significant loss is two years.

Children's reactions to loss

There are some common general reactions to loss which might include:

- behavioural problems
- aggressive behaviour
- eating/sleep disorders
- psychosomatic disorders
- attempts to replace lost person
- adopting mannerisms of lost person.

Children sometimes employ defence mechanisms which are intended to protect their self-esteem from experiences that are painful. Such defences are seen in the type of behaviours observed. They include:

- regression; for example, bedwetting
- denial
- withdrawal
- acting out – fighting
- acting in – withdrawal.

The range of emotions they are experiencing can include:

- guilt – was it something I said or did that made them go?
- anxiety – one parent has left me; will the other one leave me too?
- anger – how dare they change my life and turn my world upside down?
- sorrow – will my life ever be the same again?

Their pain displays itself through changes in their behaviour at school such as:

- learning difficulties
- restlessness
- daydreaming, poor concentration
- withdrawal
- peer relationship difficulties
- over-sensitivity to criticism
- deterioration in achievement
- delinquency.

It is important to note that basically any change in a child's normal pattern of behaviour can be a reaction to loss. There are no definitive symptoms; we each grieve in our own unique way. Our reactions to loss may be seen as a 'healing process'. Just as when we cut ourselves there is a process by which our body heals itself, so it is with emotional pain.

There is no cure for the pain that children experience. Our aim in offering help is to enable them to develop age-appropriate understanding that what they are feeling is a normal reaction. When children have intense emotional reactions it can be very scary: 'Is it normal to feel like this?' Our role can be to help them to face the painful reality at their own pace – not ours.

> **REMEMBER**
> **WHENEVER A CHILD COMPLAINS OF PHYSICAL SYMPTOMS**
> **YOU SHOULD SEEK MEDICAL ADVICE.**

2 Listening to troubled children

Before exploring some of the skills we need in order to truly listen to children we need to be aware of the many factors which will influence the type of response a child has to loss. The more we can appreciate these, the more we can appreciate the complexity of a child's reactions.

Within-child factors

As a child's thinking abilities develop, the understanding they have of loss and death affects the way in which we talk to them. We need to provide information at a level that makes sense to them. Some of the factors that will affect a child's reaction to loss are:

- age
- personality
- gender
- previous experiences
- closeness of relationship
- type of loss – sudden vs. anticipated
- expression of 'farewell'.

Listening and talking

Listening and talking to troubled children is something that we can all do. The following is intended as an *aide-mémoire* to the core skills that can help encourage a troubled child to talk to us and enable us to listen more effectively.

Do

- answer those questions that are asked
- answer questions immediately
- accept their feelings
- accept answers given
- if you don't know, say so
- say, 'Would you like to talk? I'll listen.'
- talk about feelings of guilt – 'If only'
- keep decision-making to a minimum
- remember special days; send a note
- help organise evenings and weekends with clubs and trips to ensure they have a focus and not just unstructured free time.

Avoid

- asking 'Do you understand?'
- asking multiple questions
- interrupting
- using closed questions
- saying, 'I know how you feel'
- platitudes – 'You'll get over it in time.'

Children will often be confused and frightened by the emotions they are feeling. Let them know that other children would feel the same. It can be reassuring for a child to know that their emotions are normal.

Soften painful questions. Instead of asking, 'Why did you run out of class?' ask, 'What has happened to make you upset enough to run out of class?'

Give alternatives. 'Some children like to be alone when they are sad; some children want to be with someone else when they are sad. What do you like to do when you are sad?'

Avoid forcing children to deny some undesirable behaviour. Instead of asking, 'Have you ever thought of hurting your sister?' say, 'Tell me about a time when you thought of hurting someone else.'

Allow children the chance to express positive answers before negative ones. 'What do you like best about your new class?' Follow this with 'What do you like least about your new class?'

CASE STUDY: EMMA

Emma is 11 years old and considered by most staff to be immature for her age. In class Emma is generally quiet and mixes with a few close friends. Emma's father had been terminally ill for some time and within the last week died. Since then staff have noticed that Emma is more withdrawn than usual and prone to overreacting to any form of criticism about her work. Her friends have reported that she is very sullen, moody and has been snappy with one of her closest friends.

There is a positive relationship between home and school. Emma has one brother younger than her.

Behaviour in school

Emma is seen by a number of teachers as giving cause for concern. In class her concentration span is poor and most of the time she seems unhappy, depressed and anxious. When confronted about her difficulties she will become snappy and defensive.

Observational information

Whenever we interview a child there is a lot of information available, indicated by their:

- general appearance – are they cared for? Do they care for themselves?
- speech and language – are they able to understand and express ideas?

- interaction skills – does their behaviour indicate social confidence?
- non-verbal information – do they speak with a nervous/depressed/ happy or aggressive tone?

The interview

Phase 1

Emma was clearly distressed at having to talk about her recent bereavement and half expected to be told off about her behaviour. Her helper decides to let her sit quietly and uses a 'sentence completion' task as a way of getting to know her better and to help her relax.

Some examples used are:

- I like it when ....
- One thing I like about myself is ....
- My friends like me because ....
- A happy memory I have is of when...................
- My favourite colour is.....................................
- A new skill I have learned is............................
- My favourite meal is ....

Phase 2

The child tells her story

The helper now asks Emma to tell her something about how she would like to be supported during this time in school. Emma is now more settled and begins to explain how much she hates being made to feel different because of her dad's death. It seems that everybody is asking her how she feels all the time. The helper responds with nods and such expressions as 'Ah-ha', 'Uh-hm', 'Yes' or 'Right'. Occasionally she says, 'I see what you mean' or 'I understand.'

At one point Emma says, 'I sometimes feel so angry when my friends tell me I'll be better soon. I know they're only trying to help but it stresses me out.'

The helper replies, 'You sound very frustrated and angry at everyone talking to you about your dad's death and you wish they would leave you alone.' The helper is checking with Emma that she understands what has been said. She is not repeating back what has been said in a parrot-like fashion. She is highlighting some of the key points that have been made.

Later Emma says that most of the time when she arrives home from school there is no one there, her mother having gone to fetch her little brother. It feels sometimes that he has all the time with Mum and that she is left out. The helper responds, 'It sounds as if your mum isn't around for you very often.'

Like most of us, children would often prefer to avoid exploring painful feelings. Therefore, while some children will be open, many will seek to avoid painful memories. The more we are tuned in to a child then the easier it is for us to detect their feelings. If we correctly pick up their key feelings we can help them consciously to recognise how they are feeling. It is through increasing the child's awareness and understanding that they are able to learn to accept their negative feelings and to find more positive ways of controlling and/or expressing them.

These two processes can be combined. For example, when Emma says, 'At home it's always my little brother who gets the attention; it isn't fair', the helper says, 'It sounds as if it makes you angry to see your mum giving more time to his needs than to yours.'

There are times when Emma seems to get stuck in telling her story. At such times the helper tries to help by prompting Emma to give a full description such as, 'Tell me some of the happy memories you have of your dad,' rather than asking questions that just lead to 'yes' or 'no' answers. When the helper asks, 'If you could say one thing to your dad, what would it be?' Emma responds very quickly with 'Sorry'. Further exploration shows that Emma's dad died after she woke him up playing her music. For Emma, if she hadn't done this he might still be alive.

It is not uncommon for children to implicate themselves in such painful events. They reverse to a magical thinking stage. This is the tendency for children to believe that they can make things happen just by thinking about them, or that any event that follows an action of theirs is caused by them. Thus the death of Emma's father followed her waking him up.

At times the helper feels overwhelmed by the amount of information Emma is offering and she tries to draw the key points that are being made together. 'It seems to me, Emma, that there are two main concerns that are troubling you. Firstly, at home you don't feel you are being treated as fairly or receiving as much attention from your mum as your brother is and, secondly, you feel guilty about waking your dad up on the day he died. Have I missed anything out?'

The helper is now able to focus attention on helping Emma to manage her irrational thoughts about the cause of her dad's death, and she plans to meet with Mum to improve the support Emma is receiving at home.

A MODEL OF CHANGE
Listening to children

When we are working with children it is good if we have some kind of mental template to help us support them more effectively. This can prevent us from going around in circles and feeling at a loss as to what we should do next. The model below is a template. It will not always fit your approach but it may help you keep focused.

Phase 1

Joining together
This is the stage where a relationship is developed to enable the child to feel safe and secure. Being at the same eye level as the child will be less threatening; sitting alongside rather than directly opposite is less confrontational. Using a similar response speed to the child when speaking will also help develop an emotionally supportive atmosphere.

Phase 2

Story-telling

Now the child begins to tell their story. They may do this through language, through playing with toys, drawing or puppets. Your task is to help them find the media that suits them.

Phase 3

Awareness and insight

This will obviously depend on the cognitive ability of the child. But if you can help a child develop insight into the causes of their difficulties then this will help in their motivation to change. The child here is in touch with strong negative emotions. In this phase you will help the child challenge negative self-beliefs they may have as well as understanding that their emotions are normal. Children who experience several rejections can come to believe that they are unlovable. This can be gently challenged by exploring their existing friendships and discussing the positive qualities that their friends see in them.

Phase 4

Options and choices

The child can now be helped to look for solutions or ways of coping more effectively. It is helpful to look at what they might have already tried. Often children have the right solution but don't persist with it. For example, a child might have asked a friend to come for tea one evening and, because their friend was unable to – due to existing commitments – they feel rejected and give up trying.

Phase 5

Practice

Make sure the child has time and opportunities to practise the new thinking or behavioural skills needed. Remember they may be trying to break over-learned patterns of behaviour that have helped them cope.

Such behaviours could include avoiding certain situations or people or becoming more passive and withdrawn. Habits do not change just because we wish them to.

Phase 6

Adaptive functioning
Your meetings with the child have successfully enabled them to understand why they felt like they did and why they behaved as they did. They now have better ways of coping with their thoughts and feelings.

> **REMEMBER**
> **RESISTANCE, WITHDRAWAL, AVOIDANCE AND DENIAL ARE NORMAL.**

As you help to bring issues into a child's awareness, strong negative emotions could well emerge, such as:

- sadness about the loss
- anger through rejection or envy
- anxiety through fear of loneliness.

While many children will have the psychological ability to face these emotions and to take control through understanding them, there will also be many who will block them off. When this happens it may help to change the medium that you are using. For example, they may not be able to tell their story through words. Explore alternatives, such as music, poetry, play, art, etc. Kuli, for example, was very keen on music and this was used to explore his emotions by finding songs that related to his sadness and his anger. Alternatively, if the young person follows a TV soap, then there may well be characters that they identify with and these can be used to help explore their feelings and attitudes in a way that makes sense to them. Your aim is to find a means of enabling the child to join with you to tell their story.

(Note: always remember that we are trying to be a skilled helper not a trained bereavement counsellor or Relate counsellor. The more uncertainty you feel about your role the more you should talk with colleagues. Referring on is not a sign of weakness but one of strength – it reflects your genuine care for the child.)

To conclude this chapter there are some final but extremely important points to be made.

Firstly, it is the children who are facing the loss – not us. They will cope through finding those ways that are appropriate for them.

Secondly, they are not sick or disturbed. They are facing what humanity has faced throughout all time. We suffer from an over-professionalisation of core human experiences – they have been taken over by experts. There is a risk of us talking about the children's need for therapy or counselling when in reality they need someone to help them find their way on their journey. We do not need formal training to listen in a caring and supportive way to a child in distress – if we do need formal therapy we have allowed ourselves to be deskilled in our ability to care for each other.

A child who has lost someone they cared for is in search of making sense of a new world, a world without the loved one. They need support, not therapy.

3   Bereavement

Children's understanding of death

How children respond to the death of a parent will depend on many factors, some of which have already been detailed in Chapter 1. The child's cognitive level of understanding of death is, though, one of the most important factors and will significantly determine their reactions. The role of the media cannot be underestimated in this area; many children will be seeing and learning about death via the TV soaps.

The different levels of understanding about death can be broadly assumed by age:

Birth to seven

For the very young death is synonymous with 'away' or 'out of sight, out of mind'. Providing the child has someone else they are attached to then the loss can be minimised. A child's love is not finite – they can be attached to many people.

However, during this stage the child has 'magical thinking'. Their egocentricism leads them to believe that they can make things happen – just by thinking. They can as a result have irrational thoughts which can cause emotional difficulties. For example, if a grandparent dies after an argument with a child, the child can feel responsible. Similarly they may think that they can wish someone alive again.

Seven to adolescence

Children now become more aware of the finality of death. A child's ability to deal with the severe emotional pain of loss is far less than an adult's. As a result they may:

- deny the hurt and show opposite feelings, seem to be happy
- displace their painful feelings on to another less significant event, they may overreact to the death of a pet, allowing the release of their pain
- have obsessional thoughts to do with death and funerals, etc.; for example, may visit a grave frequently and talk of joining the loved one
- have aggressive outbursts that release emotions and generate attention
- isolate themselves and withdraw from usual activities
- develop emotional and physical symptoms, such as anxiety at going to school, headaches and a loss of appetite.

Behavioural reactions

Children will often try various ways of coping, some of which are less than helpful over a long period.

- *substitution* – a child may strongly and quickly attach to a substitute mother or father
- *aggression* – a child may become unmanageable at home and fight and truant at school; a general pattern of discipline and antisocial problems may begin to emerge
- *withdrawal* – a child may lose their drive and curiosity towards life in general; their learning suffers and they develop a poor self-esteem and a 'what's the point?' attitude; they can become apathetic and socially isolated.

Why is grieving healthy?

Strong feelings of attachment and fear of abandonment are part of our biological inheritance. Through experiencing the mixture of emotions that loss causes, anger as well as sadness, we are able to move on to develop adaptive ways of coping.

What is complicated grief?

Sometimes powerful emotions are held within. When any relationship ends there are often mixed emotions. If the child has learned to suppress certain emotions, 'be strong, don't cry', they may try to suppress their feelings. But feelings do not go away – they seek release either through behaviour or physical symptoms. These emotional knots will require professional help.

When should I refer on?

Some of the signs that should lead us to referring on include when a bereaved child:

- is acting as if nothing has happened
- denies that anyone has died
- threatens or talks of suicide
- becomes persistently aggressive
- becomes withdrawn and socially isolated
- becomes involved in antisocial behaviour – drugs, stealing, etc.

> **REMEMBER**
> **IF SUICIDE WAS THE CAUSE OF DEATH, THIS CAN BE ESPECIALLY DIFFICULT FOR A CHILD TO UNDERSTAND AND COPE WITH.**

How can schools help?

Most children have a fear of being made to feel different. They have a strong desire to be similar to their peers. Any support needs to be sensitive and aware of this. A child who is grieving has the following tasks:

- to accept the loss
- to express his or her feelings

- to accept his or her feelings as normal
- to live independently without the loved one.

Returning to school after a bereavement can be stressful for children. While for some school can offer both relief and security from an overwhelmingly painful atmosphere of home, for others it increases their anxiety about the grieving parent left, perhaps alone, at home. A grieving child will be wondering how their peers and teachers are going to react to them.

Helping a child return to school after a bereavement

The skilled helper supports a child from the stage they have reached with regard to their emotions and self-understanding. Help is:

- not assuming that a child can cope without support
- being open, honest and available but not pushy
- talking about good and bad memories
- accepting a child's feelings
- writing poems, letters or songs to the loved one
- drawing pictures, or making up stories about/for the loved one
- going over final farewells, or establishing some final goodbye
- being a good listener, being there if needed
- accepting all questions without feeling the need to answer the unanswerable ones – 'I don't know' is an honest answer
- offering time to be with the child; brief but regular meetings can mean a lot to a child and being offered help is the best antidote to the fear of loneliness and rejection which a child may be feeling
- helping the child to find those friends who can be supportive
- removing unnecessary responsibilities
- modelling healthy coping strategies
- avoiding clichés such as 'You've got to be strong', 'You seem to be coping so well', 'You're the man of the house now', etc.

Ongoing support

Because all children are different and the cultures of their schools will differ also, there can be no checklist of 'things to do'. What feels right for one child in one school might not for another. The additional ideas presented here reflect this:

- establish peer support by asking the child if they have a close friend they would like to be with
- use literature, music and poetry to help a child develop an awareness and understanding of the normal human responses to pain and loss
- give permission for child to express feelings – tears are OK
- give time and attention
- listen
- tackle the taboo by being open and prepared to discuss death and family breakdown in assemblies and during circle time. If there are 'sad' events known to many children, then ensure that these are formally recognised and respected
- watch for behaviour changes
- involve child's special friends
- be honest in answering their questions
- don't deny their viewpoint
- be mindful of special days
- be aware of previous bereavements
- maintain self-esteem by encouraging the continuation of routines – seeing friends, etc.
- provide bolt-holes, such as a place in the library, where the child can go to
- keep child with peers
- be sensitive to a child's beliefs
- offer concentration strategies
- do picture stories; if a child is happy drawing, then support them in recreating special memories of holidays and trips, for example
- create a special album which could include a wide range of memories and photographs
- let them know that their thoughts and feelings are normal

- form a support circle open to all children, where an understanding of loss and our emotional reactions could be taught and ways of coping developed
- make a memorial, perhaps by creating a flower-bed or planting a tree
- encourage them to keep a journal to help them deal with their feelings
- write an account which could be shared if they chose to
- encourage them to join a local support group, such as CRUSE.

REMEMBER
ALWAYS KEEP IN TOUCH WITH THE FAMILY.

The best way to support any child is to listen and be guided by how they would like to be supported.

4 Family separation

Being brought up by a single parent, Mum or Dad, is not in itself a problem for children. For many it can be a positive experience. It is how the family breaks down and how the parents relate to each other after the separation that matters most. Twenty-eight per cent of the calls received by ChildLine are from children whose parents are not getting on well. Children are affected by family discord in a number of ways:

• they become distressed by the negative feelings it causes in them
• they become aggressive as they imitate their parents' behaviour
• they become unmanageable as a way of distracting their parents from their conflict.

Each of these has implications for how children behave in school. An indirect impact on children stems from the way in which problems between the adults can spill over into problems in the parent–child relationship. Parents caught up in hostile relationships may turn their anger towards their children. Their parenting skills are also likely to be under stress. Children may also relate back in a reciprocal manner to their parents.

SEPARATION = CHANGE

When families break down children experience many changes. Some are of a practical kind. Separation might mean:

• moving house
• changing school – having to make new friends
• new routines
• a different standard of living
• losing touch with extended family and friends

- remaining parent may now work
- new responsibilities at home.

Also separation can cause emotional changes, such as:

- feeling very sad
- becoming very angry
- missing one parent
- wanting to blame someone
- anxiety about the future
- worry about departed parent
- fear of being left by remaining parent
- coping with parents' emotions and behaviours
- divided loyalties.

Separation is an adult solution to the problem of an unhappy relationship. But from a child's point of view the adult is not just leaving his or her partner, they are leaving the family. Children can have many questions:

- where has Mummy/Daddy gone?
- why did they split up?
- will they be able to cope on their own?
- will they ever come back?
- was it my fault?
- do they still love me?
- is divorce catching – will it happen to me?
- will they still love me if they find a new partner and have new children?

Some of the emotional reactions a child might experience when a family is breaking up include:

Phase 1. Uncertainty

Family stability is threatened by discord. Children are unsure as to what will happen to them. They can feel forced to keep family secrets. They may be passive observers or become actively involved.

Emotional distress

There can be a reawakening of a child's separation anxiety from early childhood. They can have mood swings.

School behaviour

They can become over-sensitive to criticism. Their ability to concentrate diminishes and their learning will begin to suffer as emotional energy is diverted to protect self and others.

Phase 2. Denial

Children can now feel torn between their loyalties to each parent. They will act 'as if' matters were OK. They will not wish to talk about difficulties as this will make them real. They will manifest aspects of magical thinking: 'If I don't talk about it, it is not happening.'

Emotional distress

Children can experience feelings of guilt about whether or not they caused their parents to separate. Self-punishment can occur in the form of self-injurious behaviour, such as cutting, scratching and bruising themselves. The pain seems to give relief from the pain inside. Their distress can lead to nightmares as well as a lack of self-care, poor appetite, etc.

School behaviour

There might be a tendency to become isolated from others, to have little energy for new ventures and to avoid taking on responsibilities.

Phase 3. Anger

The fear of being seen to be different from others, along with a change in personal status, can lead to strong expressions of anger. They can become hostile towards the perceived guilty parent.

Emotional distress

Pent-up anger may be turned outwards by showing anger towards other children; this is in effect envy at their apparent happy family lives. Or the anger can be turned in on the self in the form of extreme submissiveness, as seen in the child who no longer initiates conversations with friends and seems to expect to be left out of activities.

School behaviour

Children can become emotionally volatile and prone to sudden outbursts in the classroom. Small frustrations trigger off excessive reactions.

Phase 4. Despair

There is a loss of pleasure in activities that they used to enjoy. They may no longer enjoy their usual TV programmes and they respond coolly to trips that were once welcomed. There is a realisation that reunion of their family is unlikely. The child's growing sense of acceptance brings grief-like reactions.

Emotional distress

There is a tendency for children in this phase to suffer psychosomatic illnesses such as stomach pains and headaches – as if they search for increased nurture. Regressive behaviours such as bedwetting and clinginess may also emerge. Again, these are behaviours that seek to elicit increased support at a time of sorrow.

School behaviour

Responses more appropriate to the child when younger can develop. They may cry at minor setbacks and run out of lessons when reprimanded.

Phase 5. Coping

The child is now coming to terms with a new 'normality'. They have acquired a new identity.

Emotional distress
There can be apprehensiveness about a parent developing new relationships.

School behaviour
They develop a more open-minded approach and a willingness to explore alternative solutions and become less rigid in their thinking, returning to their thinking style prior to the loss. They are more optimistic about the future and will, for example, be less critical of the parent who left the family home.

Supporting children in school

When talking with children it is important to bear in mind that their reactions to separation vary according to their age and the support they are given should be appropriate to their level of development.

Reactions and support by age

Preschool
Children of this age have limited understanding and will often escape into fantasy. They may regress and lose skills they had mastered. Bedwetting may start and nightmares are not uncommon. They may show signs of anxiety about meeting the other parent. Their sleep and eating patterns might change.

At this age children need brief and clear instructions and explanations. Routines are very important and extra comforters such as cuddles and security toys matter a lot.

Primary
Children now experience worries about losing their family. They can experience intense sadness and they can also feel angry at being left by one parent. They can become involved in taking messages between their parents. In school they can become disorganised and may be aggressive towards authority figures.

Questions now need to be answered sensitively and regular opportunities made to allow the child to talk if he or she wishes.

Secondary

Children can now become extremely embarrassed about the change in their family. They often have strong ideas about right and wrong and may well see one parent as being to blame. They may cope by throwing themselves into schoolwork or activities as a way of avoiding the painful reality.

Children need to have their worries accepted and to be reassured that their reactions are normal. Any behavioural problems need to be treated in a matter-of-fact manner.

General

All children will suffer from a sense of helplessness. They are at risk of feeling out of control and that nothing they do can make a difference; for example, when parents try to involve them in arrangements they seem uninterested. While there are many aspects of separation that are naturally beyond their control it is important to help children appreciate those aspects of their lives where they do have control, such as organising their weekend activities, meeting with friends, clothes, etc.

Further reading

References

Holmes, J. (1995) *John Bowlby and Attachment Theory*. London: Routledge.

Robertson, J. (1952) Film: *A Two-Year-Old Goes to Hospital*. London: Tavistock.

Recommended reading

Atkinson, M. and Hornby, G. (2002) *Mental Health Handbook for Schools*. London: Routledge Falmer.

Ayalon, O. and Flasher, A. (1993) *Chain Reaction: Children and Divorce*. London: Jessica Kingsley Publishers.

Boyd Webb, N. (1993) *Helping Bereaved Children*. New York: The Guilford Press.

Cox, K. and Desforges, M. (1987) *Divorce and the School*. London: Methuen.

James, J. and Friedman, R. (2001) *When Children Grieve*. New York: HarperCollins Publishers.

Jewett, C. (1982) *Helping Children Cope with Separation and Loss*. London: Batsford.

Reynolds, J. (2001) *Not in Front of the Children?* London: One Plus One.

Sharp, S. and Cowie, H. (1998) *Counselling and Supporting Children in Distress*. London: SAGE.

Contacts

CRUSE: a charitable organisation offering bereavement counselling, training workshops and publications.

www:crusebereavementcare.org.uk

helpline: 0870 167 1677